THE MIRROR EFFECT
Workbook & Journal

DR. SHEILA GUJRATHI

the MIRROR EFFECT
Workbook & Journal

GROWTH EXERCISES *for the*
NEXT GENERATION *of* **FEMALE LEADERS**

an imprint of Amplify Publishing Group

www.amplifypublishinggroup.com

The Mirror Effect Workbook & Journal:
Growth Exercises for the Next Generation of Female Leaders

©2025 Dr. Sheila Gujrathi. All Rights Reserved. No part of this publication may be reproduced, stored in a retrieval system or transmitted in any form by any means electronic, mechanical, or photocopying, recording or otherwise without the permission of the author.

The views and opinions expressed in this book are solely those of the author. These views and opinions do not necessarily represent those of the publisher or staff. The publisher and the author assume no responsibility for errors, inaccuracies, omissions, or any other inconsistencies herein. All such instances are unintentional and the author's own.

For more information, please contact:
Amplify Publishing, an imprint of Amplify Publishing Group
620 Herndon Parkway, Suite 220
Herndon, VA 20170
info@amplifypublishing.com

CPSIA Code: PRV0825A

ISBN-13: 979-8-89138-781-2

Printed in the United States

This workbook and journal is dedicated to you on your journey.

CONTENTS

A LETTER TO YOU   ix

INTRODUCTION
Preparing the Days (Days 1–7)   xi

CHAPTER 1
It's Time: Reclaiming Your Vision and Voice (Days 8–14)   1

CHAPTER 2
**How to Become Unshakable: Naming Fear,
Insecurity, Doubt, and Shame (Days 15-21)**   19

CHAPTER 3
**The Four Archetypes:
Breaking Through the Inner Glass Ceiling (Days 22-28)**   39

CHAPTER 4
**Powerful Beyond Measure:
Seeing—and Being—Your Best Self (Days 29-35)**   59

CHAPTER 5
**Uncharted Territory:
Navigating Difficult Work Environments (Days 36-42)**   81

CHAPTER 6
**Tyrants and Rivals and Deceivers (Oh My!):
Working with Wounded People (Days 43-49)**   99

CHAPTER 7
The Gift of Misperception: Assessing and Addressing the Ways You're Perceived (Days 50-56)   117

CHAPTER 8
When You Know, You Know: Finding an Environment Where You Can Thrive (Days 57-63)   135

CHAPTER 9
Surround Yourself with Mirrors: Building Your Personal Board of Directors (Days 64-70)   153

CHAPTER 10
Master Negotiations: Getting What You Want Without Compromising Yourself (Days 71-77)   171

CHAPTER 11
Harness Your Presence:
Managing Your Energy to Level Up (Days 78–84)   189

CONCLUSION
Be Bold: Realizing Your Dreams (Days 85–90)   207

FINAL REFLECTIONS   223

ABOUT THE AUTHOR   225

A LETTER TO YOU

Dear Reader,

I created this workbook because I've witnessed too many brilliant, talented professionals diminish themselves or become trapped in environments that don't recognize their worth. I've experienced this myself. But you've already taken the first step in getting free of the conditioning that's held you back and breaking through the internal and external glass ceilings that have threatened to keep you down. Congratulations on choosing yourself! I'm honored to be by your side as you take this journey.

This workbook is both a mirror and a map. It offers ninety days' worth of prompts to take you on a transformative exploration of your professional identity, working environment, and personal power. Keep in mind, though, that this isn't meant to be prescriptive. This workbook is here to foster *your* growth. If you want to respond to the same prompt for five days or blast through ten prompts in a single sitting, that's great. If you step away for a month to embark on another self-discovery journey or simply to take a break, perfect. Take it at your own pace, and use it to get what you need.

A Letter to You

As you progress through these pages (regardless of when or how long it takes), you'll begin to see yourself more clearly—perhaps for the first time—and chart a course toward your most authentic and empowered self.

The prompts within these pages are drawn from years of mentoring leaders who felt sidelined, undervalued, or unable to fully express their authentic selves. They reflect the real challenges we face and the genuine breakthroughs that are possible when we commit to self-reflection and growth.

While I'll always be by your side on the page, consider going through the workbook with a friend, peer group, or book club—there's so much you can learn and build when you don't go it alone.

My hope is that this workbook becomes a trusted companion as you navigate your professional journey—a place where you can be completely honest with yourself, where you can recognize patterns that no longer serve you, and where you can begin to envision and create a future aligned with your true power and potential.

With admiration and belief in your journey,

 P.S. If you haven't watched my TEDx Talk on The Mirror Effect, "Shattering the Glass Ceiling by Finding the Right Mirrors," you can check it out here!

INTRODUCTION
PREPARING THE DAYS
(Days 1–7)

> "You alone are enough. You have nothing to prove to anybody."
>
> –*Maya Angelou*

DAY 1: SETTING INTENTIONS

Reflect on what drew you to this workbook. What specific challenges are you facing in your professional life? What hopes do you have for your journey through these pages?

_____

_____

_____

_____

_____

_____

DAY 2: YOUR PROFESSIONAL STORY

Write about your professional journey to date. What pivotal moments have shaped your career path? Which achievements make you proud? What patterns do you notice in retrospect?

_____

_____

_____

_____

_____

_____

_____

_____

_____

_____

_____

Introduction

Introduction

DAY 3: TAKING STOCK

Make an honest assessment of where you stand today professionally. What strengths do you bring to your work? Where do you feel unseen or undervalued? What aspects of your professional life energize or drain you?

_____

_____

_____

_____

_____

_____

_____

_____

_____

_____

_____

DAY 4: ACKNOWLEDGING BARRIERS

Consider the external and internal barriers you've encountered. How have societal expectations, workplace culture, or personal beliefs limited your professional growth? Which barriers feel most significant?

_____

_____

_____

_____

_____

_____

_____

_____

_____

_____

_____

_____

Introduction

DAY 5: YOUR PROFESSIONAL IDENTITY

How do you currently see yourself as a professional? What labels do you embrace or reject? How does your professional identity connect to your authentic self?

_____

_____

_____

_____

_____

_____

_____

_____

_____

_____

_____

_____

Introduction

DAY 6: YOUR MIRRORS

Who has truly seen and reflected your potential throughout your career? How have these people shaped your self-perception and professional journey?

_____

_____

_____

_____

_____

_____

_____

_____

_____

_____

_____

_____

_____

DAY 7: PREPARING FOR CHANGE

As you prepare to dive deeper into self-knowledge, what resistances or fears might emerge? What would help you stay committed to this reflective practice even when it becomes challenging?

_____

_____

_____

_____

_____

_____

_____

_____

_____

_____

_____

_____

Introduction

EXERCISE: GET CLEAR ON YOUR VALUES

Before diving deeper into your professional journey, take time to identify the core values that guide your decisions and priorities.

Step 1: Identify Peak Moments: Think about three moments in your professional life when you felt most alive, fulfilled, and authentic. Briefly describe each.

1. _____
2. _____
3. _____

Step 2: Extract the Values: For each moment, ask yourself the following:

- What made this experience meaningful?
- What need or desire was being fulfilled?
- What principles were being honored?

From these reflections, identify potential core values (e.g., authenticity, creativity, impact, connection, growth, recognition).

Step 3: Narrow Your Focus: Review your list and circle the three to five values that most strongly resonate with you.

1. _____
2. _____
3. _____

4. _____
5. _____

Step 4: Test Your Values: For each value, ask the following:

- Would I stand by this value even if it came at a cost?
- Does this value consistently guide my decisions?
- Would I want to be known for embodying this value?

Step 5: Create Value Definitions: Write a personal definition for each core value that captures what it specifically means to you.

Value: _____
My definition: _____

Step 6: Check Values Alignment: Rate how well your current professional life allows you to express each value (on a scale of 1–10).

- Value #1: _____
- Value #2: _____
- Value #3: _____

REFLECTION QUESTIONS

1. Which value feels most alive in your work right now?
2. Which value feels most suppressed or neglected?
3. What small step could you take this week to better align with your core values?

FEEL FREE TO USE THE FOLLOWING PAGES FOR ANSWERING AND REFLECTING ON THE EXERCISE QUESTIONS

CHAPTER 1

IT'S TIME
Reclaiming Your Vision and Voice (Days 8–14)

> "It took me quite a long time to develop a voice, and now that I have it, I am not going to be silent."
>
> –Madeleine Albright

DAY 8: THE SILENCED SELF

Examine a moment when you silenced your authentic self at work. What led to that choice? How would your authentic self have preferred to respond?

_____

_____

_____

_____

_____

DAY 9: ORIGIN STORIES

Write about your earliest memory of feeling like an outsider professionally. How has that experience shaped your self-perception? What aspects of that story still influence you?

_____

_____

_____

_____

_____

_____

_____

_____

_____

_____

_____

_____

DAY 10: VALUES ALIGNMENT

Map out your true priorities and values. Where do they align with your current work life? Where do they conflict? What does this reveal about changes you might need to make?

_____

_____

_____

_____

_____

_____

_____

_____

_____

_____

_____

_____

_____

_____

DAY 11: TONING DOWN

Reflect on a time when you felt pressured to "tone yourself down" at work. What parts of yourself did you feel compelled to hide? What would embracing those parts look like?

DAY 12: POWER DYNAMICS

Consider your relationship with power. When do you feel most empowered? When do you shrink? What does this reveal about your core beliefs?

DAY 13: THE INNER CRITIC

Describe your inner critic's voice when you face workplace challenges. Whose voice is it, really? How has it evolved from your early career until now?

DAY 14: CLAIMING VICTORY

Write about a professional victory you've downplayed or dismissed. Why did you minimize it? What stops you from fully owning your achievements?

_____

_____

_____

_____

_____

_____

_____

_____

_____

_____

_____

_____

EXERCISE: TAKE STOCK

Use this exercise to take stock of where you are in your career and identify patterns that may be holding you back from reaching your full potential.

PART 1: EXTERNAL ASSESSMENT

CURRENT REALITY SNAPSHOT

- My title/role: _____
- My responsibilities: _____
- What I'm known for: _____
- My recent achievements: _____
- Challenges I'm facing: _____

OPPORTUNITY ANALYSIS

- Skills I'm developing: _____
- Relationships I'm building: _____
- Visibility I'm gaining: _____
- Barriers I'm encountering: _____

PART 2: INTERNAL ASSESSMENT

Self-Talk Inventory: Write down three thoughts you frequently have about yourself professionally.

For each thought, ask the following:

1. Is this actually true? _____

2. Where did this belief come from? _____
3. How is this serving or limiting me?_____
4. What alternative thought would be more empowering?
   _____

PART 3: PATTERN RECOGNITION

Success Patterns: When have you been at your professional best? Note common elements across these experiences.

- Work environment factors: _____
- Types of tasks/projects: _____
- People you worked with: _____
- Leadership styles you responded to: _____
- How you felt physically and emotionally: _____

Struggle Patterns: When have you felt most frustrated professionally? Note common elements.

- Triggering situations: _____
- Types of people/interactions: _____
- What preceded feelings of doubt or fear: _____
- Physical and emotional indicators: _____

PART 4: INTEGRATION AND ACTION

Based on your audit, identify the following:

- Three strengths to leverage: _____
- Two patterns to disrupt: _____

- One immediate action to take: _____

Commitment: Write a specific commitment to yourself about one change you'll make this week based on what you've discovered.

Remember: Awareness is the first step toward transformation. This audit gives you valuable data about where you are now and what patterns may be influencing your professional journey. Use this information as you continue through the workbook to make conscious choices about your next steps.

_____

_____

_____

_____

FEEL FREE TO USE THE FOLLOWING PAGES FOR ANSWERING AND REFLECTING ON THE EXERCISE QUESTIONS

_____

_____

_____

_____

_____

CHAPTER 2

HOW TO BECOME UNSHAKABLE
Naming Fear, Insecurity, Doubt, and Shame (Days 15–21)

> "If you take care of your mind,
> you take care of the world."
>
> *–Arianna Huffington*

DAY 15: FACING FEAR

Describe a recent situation where fear held you back professionally. What triggered this fear? How did your body respond? What truth lies beneath this fear?

_____

_____

_____

_____

DAY 16: INSECURITY PATTERNS

Identify three recurring situations that make you feel insecure at work. For each one, explore: What old story or wound might this be touching? What would security feel like?

_____

_____

_____

_____

_____

_____

_____

_____

_____

_____

_____

_____

_____

_____

DAY 17: DOUBT TRACKING

Track your doubt patterns for a day. When does self-doubt surface? What messages do you tell yourself? Write a compassionate response to each doubt.

_____

_____

_____

_____

_____

_____

_____

_____

_____

_____

_____

_____

_____

DAY 18: SHAME STORIES

Reflect on a time when shame derailed your confidence. What triggered it? How did you internalize it? What would it look like to release this shame?

_____

_____

_____

_____

_____

_____

_____

_____

_____

_____

_____

_____

_____

DAY 19: ACHIEVEMENT AMNESIA

Write about a moment when you dismissed your achievements. Where did this response come from? What would a self-compassionate response sound like?

_____

_____

_____

_____

_____

_____

_____

_____

_____

_____

_____

_____

_____

DAY 20: IMPOSTER MOMENTS

Consider a time when you felt like an imposter. What evidence were you ignoring about your capabilities? What would it take to fully own your expertise?

DAY 21: TRIGGER MAPPING

Examine a trigger that consistently affects your professional confidence. How does it manifest physically? Emotionally? What past experience might it be connected to?

_____

_____

_____

_____

_____

_____

_____

_____

_____

_____

_____

_____

EXERCISE: NAVIGATE YOUR FIDS

Fear, insecurity, doubt, and shame (FIDS) can be powerful internal barriers to stepping into your full power. This exercise will help you identify, understand, and begin transforming these obstacles.

PART 1: FIDS IDENTIFICATION

For each component of FIDS, reflect on how it appears in your professional life.

Fear

- What situations at work consistently trigger anxiety or fear?
- What are you most afraid might happen in your career?
- How does fear show up physically in your body during challenging work situations?

Insecurity

- In what professional contexts do you feel most insecure?
- What qualities or skills do you worry you lack compared with peers?
- When do you feel the need to prove yourself or your worth?

Doubt

- What achievements or capabilities do you tend to second-guess?

- When do you find yourself hesitating to speak up or take action?
- What negative predictions do you make about outcomes when you're in doubt?

Shame

- What aspects of your professional self do you hide or diminish?
- When have you felt "exposed" or deeply embarrassed at work?
- What past mistakes still make you cringe with shame?

PART 2: PATTERN RECOGNITION

1. Review your responses and look for patterns.
2. Circle recurring themes across different FIDS components.
3. Underline specific situations that trigger multiple FIDS responses.
4. Put a star next to the FIDS reactions that most limit your professional growth.

PART 3: PHYSICAL AWARENESS PRACTICE

Choose one common triggering situation from your patterns. For one week practice this physical awareness sequence when you encounter it.

1. **Notice:** What physical sensations arise (e.g., heat in the chest, tension in the shoulders)?

2. **Name:** Silently label which FIDS component you're experiencing.
3. **Breathe:** Take three slow, deep breaths into your belly.
4. **Expand:** Consciously open your posture instead of contracting.
5. **Center:** Return attention to your breath until you feel more grounded.

Record your observations.

- Which physical cues helped you catch reactions earlier?
- What difference did conscious breathing and posture changes make?
- How did naming the experience affect your response?

PART 4: COMPASSIONATE REFRAMING

Select one persistent FIDS pattern to work with. Complete this reframing process.

1. **Name what's causing the reaction:** "I feel [fear/insecurity/doubt/shame] when _____."
2. **Challenge the narrative:** "The story I'm telling myself is _____, but that may not be true because _____."
3. **Bring in counterexamples:** "Evidence that contradicts this belief includes _____."
4. **Practice self-compassion:** "What I would say to a friend in this situation is _____."

5. **Create a power phrase:** Develop a short, powerful statement to recall when this pattern arises: "_____."

PART 5: INTEGRATION AND REFLECTION

After practicing these approaches for one week, reflect on the following:

1. Which FIDS component feels most limiting in your professional life right now?
2. What new insight did you gain about the root cause of this pattern?
3. What physical signals now help you recognize when you're being triggered?
4. Which strategy (noticing, naming, breathing, expanding, or reframing) was most helpful?
5. How has your relationship to this FIDS component shifted?
6. What situation still feels challenging, and what additional support might you need?

Commitment: Based on what you've learned, write one specific commitment to yourself about how you'll continue to address your primary FIDS challenge.

"I commit to _____."

Remember: Becoming unshakable doesn't mean never experiencing FIDS—it means developing the awareness to recognize these reactions early and the tools to respond rather than react. With practice, you'll find yourself remaining centered even when faced with situations that previously knocked you off-balance.

FEEL FREE TO USE THE FOLLOWING PAGES FOR ANSWERING AND REFLECTING ON THE EXERCISE QUESTIONS

CHAPTER 3

THE FOUR ARCHETYPES
Breaking Through the Inner Glass Ceiling (Days 22–28)

> "There's always going to be somebody telling you you don't belong and you can't do this. You've got to practice a different set of tools."
>
> –Michelle Obama

DAY 22: LEADERSHIP DEFAULT

Reflect on your default leadership style. What role do you tend to play at work—the Peacekeeper, the Perfectionist, the Authority Figure, or the Overseer? How did you develop this pattern, and what impact does it have on your effectiveness?

_____

_____

_____

_____

DAY 23: THE PEOPLE-PLEASER

Recall a time when you defaulted to people-pleasing at work. What were you afraid would happen if you didn't? What would setting a healthy boundary have looked like?

_____

_____

_____

_____

_____

_____

_____

_____

_____

_____

_____

_____

_____

DAY 24: THE IMPOSTER

Document a moment when imposter syndrome affected your decision-making. What evidence of your competence were you overlooking? What would trusting yourself have changed?

_____

_____

_____

_____

_____

_____

_____

_____

_____

_____

_____

_____

DAY 25: THE BITCH BOSS

Consider times when you've been labeled "difficult" or "bossy." How did gender or cultural expectations influence these labels? How has this affected your leadership style?

_____

_____

_____

_____

_____

_____

_____

_____

_____

_____

_____

_____

_____

DAY 26: THE MICROMANAGER

Examine your relationship with control at work. When do you feel compelled to micromanage? What fears or insecurities drive this need?

_____

_____

_____

_____

_____

_____

_____

_____

_____

_____

_____

DAY 27: FEEDBACK FILTERS

Reflect on feedback you've received about your leadership style. Which comments reflect genuine areas for growth? Which might stem from bias? How do you distinguish between them?

_____

_____

_____

_____

_____

_____

_____

_____

_____

_____

_____

_____

_____

_____

DAY 28: BREAKING PATTERNS

Write about a time when you successfully broke free from a limiting leadership pattern. What enabled the change? How did it feel? What did you learn?

_____

_____

_____

_____

_____

_____

_____

_____

_____

_____

EXERCISE: IDENTIFY YOUR ARCHETYPE

Understanding which archetype you tend to embody is the first step toward breaking free from its limitations. Let's explore some common signs of each archetype so you can better identify your own patterns.

THE PEOPLE-PLEASER

- You find it hard to refuse requests.
- You overcommit to plans, responsibilities, or projects.
- You don't advocate for your own needs.
- You go along with things you aren't happy about to avoid friction.
- You feel stressed and overwhelmed, which can result in resentment and passive-aggressive behaviors.
- You rarely complain or call out unfair treatment.
- You're afraid of punishment or reprisal.
- You struggle to hold on to your own beliefs and be true to yourself.

THE IMPOSTER

- You feel like a fraud despite evidence of your ongoing success.
- You attribute your accomplishments to external factors such as luck or timing.
- You think, *It's only a matter of time before everyone realizes I'm a fraud.*
- You believe people are only being nice to you because they feel obligated.

- You constantly feel you don't deserve your position.
- You question whether you should even be where you are.
- You judge yourself and your accomplishments harshly.
- Your mind transforms your greatest triumphs into failures.

THE BITCH BOSS

- You're seen as difficult, rude, or mean.
- You ask for more than you really want—or demand instead of asking.
- You set high—and sometimes rigid—expectations for your team members.
- You create an environment where people are afraid to ask for help.
- You don't always respect others' boundaries.
- You often surround yourself with junior people who validate your decisions.
- You may have been labeled as having "sharp elbows."
- You feel you must make others listen to you.

THE MICROMANAGER

- You ask to be copied on all team emails.
- You rarely ask for outside input.
- You take pride in correcting other people's work.
- You check, double-check, and triple-check on deadlines.
- You apply the same level of intensity to every task and struggle to prioritize.
- You're never quite satisfied with the final product.
- You don't trust others to complete tasks properly.
- You feel a need to control every aspect of a project.

The Four Archetypes

Take time to honestly assess which patterns you recognize in yourself. You may identify strongly with one archetype or see elements of several in your behavior. Remember that these archetypes aren't who you are—they're roles you've adopted, often unconsciously, in response to your conditioning and circumstances.

By recognizing these patterns, you can begin to understand the underlying FIDS that drive them. This awareness is the first step toward breaking through your inner glass ceiling and stepping into your authentic leadership style.

After identifying which archetype(s) you tend to embody, use these practical tips to help shift your patterns and behaviors:

IF YOU'RE A PEOPLE-PLEASER, TRY THESE MANTRAS

- No. (Remember: No is a complete sentence!)
- I don't have to apologize or explain myself to anyone.
- My time and energy are my own.
- Not my circus, not my monkeys.

WHEN COMMUNICATING WITH OTHERS, PRACTICE THESE PHRASES

- "I won't be able to make it."
- "Unfortunately, I'm at capacity. I'll have to pass."
- "I'll think about it and touch base with you tomorrow."
- "I have plans that day, but thank you for thinking of me."

IF YOU STRUGGLE WITH IMPOSTER SYNDROME

- Pay attention to your posture. Do you shrink yourself? Stand tall with your head high and shoulders back.
- Keep a "wins journal" to document compliments, achievements, and positive feedback.

- Before important meetings, do a "power pose" in private to boost your confidence.
- When self-doubt creeps in, ask yourself, "What evidence do I have of my competence in this area?" Focus on facts rather than feelings.
- Find an accountability partner who can remind you of your capabilities when you forget.

IF YOU'VE BEEN LABELED A BITCH BOSS OR WORRY ABOUT BEING SEEN AS TOO AGGRESSIVE

- Pair strong leadership with genuine kindness—you can be decisive without being harsh.
- Ask for specific feedback about your communication style from trusted colleagues.
- Focus on the outcome, not on controlling the process.
- Create opportunities for two-way feedback with your team.
- Remember that being respected is more valuable than being liked.
- When delivering constructive criticism, use the "feedback sandwich" method: positive comment, area for improvement, positive comment.

IF YOU TEND TO MICROMANAGE

- Set clear expectations about outcomes rather than dictating the exact process.
- Create checkpoints for feedback instead of hovering throughout projects.
- Practice pausing before intervening—ask yourself, "Is this necessary?" before stepping in.

- Start with small acts of delegation to build your trust muscle.
- Focus your attention on the most critical aspects of projects, letting go of less important details.
- Document positive outcomes when you successfully delegate to build evidence that your team can succeed without your constant oversight.
- Shifting from these archetypes isn't about changing who you are but about expanding your range so you can access your authentic power in any situation. Which small adjustment from the list above could you commit to practicing this week?

FEEL FREE TO USE THE FOLLOWING PAGES FOR ANSWERING AND REFLECTING ON THE EXERCISE QUESTIONS

CHAPTER 4

POWERFUL BEYOND MEASURE
Seeing—and Being—Your Best Self (Days 29–35)

> "Our deepest fear is not that we are inadequate. Our deepest fear is that we are powerful beyond measure."
>
> –*Marianne Williamson*

DAY 29: SELF-COMPASSION PRACTICE

Practice the self-compassion exercise from chapter 4: Write down something negative you've said to yourself recently, then imagine saying it to someone you love. Now write what you would actually say to that person in this situation. Finally, rewrite your self-talk using this compassionate language.

_____

_____

_____

DAY 30: FINDING CENTER

Reflect on a moment when you felt truly centered and at peace. What elements contributed to this feeling? What was happening in your body, your mind, and your surroundings? How might you recreate these conditions more regularly?

DAY 31: EMBRACING POWER

Consider Marianne Williamson's quote: "Our deepest fear is not that we are inadequate. Our deepest fear is that we are powerful beyond measure." When have you shied away from your own power? What would embracing your full potential look like?

DAY 32: THE THREE C'S PLAN

Create your own "Three C's" practice plan. List specific ways you can cultivate self-compassion, find your center, and celebrate yourself regularly. Which aspects feel most challenging, and why?

_____

_____

_____

_____

_____

_____

_____

_____

_____

_____

_____

_____

_____

DAY 33: CELEBRATION PRACTICE

Identify an achievement you've downplayed or kept to yourself. Why did you hesitate to celebrate it? Draft a social media post or message to friends sharing this accomplishment in a way that feels authentic to you.

_____

_____

_____

_____

_____

_____

_____

_____

_____

_____

_____

_____

DAY 34: SELF-LOVE LETTER

Write a love letter to yourself, acknowledging your strengths, growth, and resilience. What would someone who truly sees and appreciates you want you to know about yourself?

DAY 35: THE ENOUGH QUESTION

Reflect on Oprah's question: "Are you enough for yourself?" Explore your relationship with external validation versus internal worthiness. What would it look like to truly believe you are enough, just as you are?

_____

_____

_____

_____

_____

_____

_____

_____

_____

_____

_____

_____

_____

_____

EXERCISE: CELEBRATE YOURSELF

Self-celebration isn't self-indulgence—it's a powerful practice that reinforces your worth and accomplishments. This exercise will help you overcome resistance to celebrating yourself and develop a sustainable practice of acknowledging your achievements.

PART 1: CELEBRATION RESISTANCE INVENTORY

Reflect on your relationship with self-celebration by completing these statements:

1. When I accomplish something significant, I typically _____.
2. When others praise me, I usually respond by _____.
3. The last time I publicly acknowledged my own achievement was _____.
4. When I think about celebrating my successes, I worry that _____.
5. I find it easier to celebrate others when _____.

PART 2: BREAKING THROUGH BARRIERS

For each barrier to self-celebration you identified, challenge it directly.

Barrier: "I don't want to seem arrogant or self-centered."

Reframe: "Acknowledging my achievements demonstrates my value and can inspire others."

Evidence: Think of someone whose success inspired you. Did you view them as arrogant?

___

Barrier: "Others might think I'm bragging."

Reframe: "Celebrating accomplishments creates a culture where everyone can acknowledge their worth."

Practice: Write three ways to authentically share a victory that feels comfortable to you.

Barrier: "My achievement isn't that special."

Reframe: "Every step forward deserves recognition, especially in the face of challenges."

Reality check: Would you diminish this same achievement if a friend accomplished it?

___

Barrier (Write your own): _____

_____

_____

Reframe: _____

_____

_____

Challenge: _____

_____

_____

PART 3: CELEBRATION INVENTORY

Create a comprehensive list of your recent achievements—both big and small.

- **Professional wins (last six months)**
- **Personal growth milestones**
- **Challenges overcome**
- **Values I've honored through my actions**

Circle one achievement from each category that you haven't fully acknowledged or celebrated.

PART 4: CELEBRATION PRACTICE DESIGN

Create your personalized celebration practice.

Social media celebration plan:

- Platform I'm most comfortable sharing on: _____
  _____
- Type of achievements I'll share: _____
  Frequency (e.g., monthly, quarterly): _____
  _____
- My authentic sharing style: _____
- Draft post for your next achievement: _____
  _____

Private celebration rituals:

- Solo celebration activity: _____
- People to share wins with: _____
- Physical reminder of achievements (e.g., journal, visual board): _____
- Reward system for milestones: _____

PART 5: MIRROR CREATION

Just as you can be a mirror for others, create a system for others to reflect your achievements back to you.

- Identify three to five people who can serve as your "celebration circle."
- Share this intention with them: "I'm working on acknowledging my achievements more openly. Would you be willing to help reflect back my successes when you notice them?"

- Create a mechanism for celebration (e.g., group text, regular check-ins).
- Commit to being a celebration mirror for them in return.

PART 6: WEEKLY CELEBRATION PRACTICE

1. For one week implement this daily celebration ritual.
2. Each evening write down one thing you accomplished or did well that day.
3. Acknowledge how this achievement aligns with your values or goals.
4. Take thirty seconds to physically celebrate (e.g., a victory dance, power pose).
5. Share at least one achievement (small or large) publicly during the week.
6. Notice how celebration affects your energy and confidence.

REFLECTION QUESTIONS

1. What physical sensations did you notice when celebrating your achievements?
2. How did others respond when you shared your accomplishments?
3. Which celebration practices felt most authentic and energizing?
4. What surprised you about the experience of intentional self-celebration?
5. How might regular self-celebration affect your professional presence and power?

6. What continuing practice will you commit to moving forward?

Commitment: "I deserve to be celebrated. I commit to acknowledging my achievements by _____."

Remember: Self-celebration isn't about inflating your ego—it's about accurately recognizing your contributions and worth. When you acknowledge your accomplishments, you not only reinforce your own value but also create permission for others to do the same. Your celebrations create ripples that empower everyone around you.

FEEL FREE TO USE THE FOLLOWING PAGES FOR ANSWERING AND REFLECTING ON THE EXERCISE QUESTIONS

_____

_____

_____

_____

_____

_____

_____

CHAPTER 5

UNCHARTED TERRITORY
Navigating Difficult Work Environments (Days 36–42)

> "The most rage-provoking element of being a female is the gaslighting that happens when for centuries we've been expected to absorb male behavior silently."
>
> –*Taylor Swift*

DAY 36: SAFETY SIGNALS

Reflect on a time when you felt psychologically unsafe at work. What specific behaviors or interactions triggered this feeling? How did your body and mind respond to the environment?

_____

_____

_____

_____

DAY 37: GASLIGHTING EXPERIENCE

Describe a moment when you witnessed or experienced workplace gaslighting. What made you doubt your own perception? What internal dialogue accompanied those doubts?

_____

_____

_____

_____

_____

_____

_____

_____

_____

_____

_____

DAY 38: TOXIC COMPETITION

Write about a time when workplace competition turned toxic. How did the environment affect your performance, mental health, and sense of self? What survival strategies did you develop?

DAY 39: FEAR-BASED CULTURE

Examine a situation where fear dominated your workplace culture. How did this fear manifest? What unspoken rules were you expected to follow? How did you compromise your authenticity to survive?

DAY 40: OUTSIDER EXPERIENCE

Recall an instance when you felt like an outsider in a professional setting. What cultural, racial, or gender dynamics contributed to your isolation? How did these dynamics shape your behavior and self-perception?

DAY 41: SILENCING MECHANISMS

Reflect on a time when you were silenced or overlooked in a professional environment. What mechanisms of power were at play? How did you internalize this experience?

DAY 42: COMPROMISE ASSESSMENT

Consider a moment when you chose to stay in a challenging work environment. What compromises did you make? What parts of yourself did you have to hide or minimize to belong?

EXERCISE: THREE SMART STEPS FOR NAVIGATING TOXIC ENVIRONMENTS

When you find yourself in a challenging workplace, you need a practical approach to protect yourself and determine your next move. Here are three strategic steps to take:

1. RECOGNIZE REALITY

- Trust your instincts when something feels off.
- Document specific incidents, dates, and patterns.
- Ask yourself honestly, "Do I feel safe and supported here?"
- Acknowledge how you're feeling without self-blame.

2. GATHER SUPPORT

- Identify two to three trusted colleagues who can provide perspective.
- Reach out to your personal board members outside the organization.
- Ask specific questions such as "Have you noticed this behavior?" or "Am I reading this situation correctly?"
- Share your experiences with someone who can offer objective insight.

3. MAKE YOUR MOVE

- Prepare thoroughly before any confrontation.
- List specific examples with dates.
- Practice what you'll say.

- Anticipate possible responses.
- Request a formal meeting rather than an impromptu conversation.
- Use clear "I" statements during the conversation.
- Set concrete next steps and timelines.
- Watch closely for what happens after your conversation.
- Be prepared to walk away if necessary.

REFLECTION QUESTIONS

1. Which of these steps feels most challenging to you, and why?
2. What specific evidence have you collected about your current environment?
3. Who are the people you trust to give you honest feedback?
4. What would be your first concrete step if you decide action is needed?

You deserve an environment that recognizes your worth. Sometimes the most powerful move is walking away from toxicity toward an opportunity that allows you to thrive.

FEEL FREE TO USE THE FOLLOWING PAGES FOR ANSWERING AND REFLECTING ON THE EXERCISE QUESTIONS

CHAPTER 6
TYRANTS AND RIVALS AND DECEIVERS (OH MY!)
Working with Wounded People (Days 43–49)

> "You can't control how other people receive your energy. Anything you do or say gets filtered through the lens of whatever personal stuff they are dealing with at the moment."
>
> —Mel Robbins

DAY 43: THE TYRANT

Reflect on a time when you encountered a workplace "tyrant." What power dynamics were at play? How did their behavior make you question your own worth or capabilities?

_____

_____

_____

_____

DAY 44: THE RIVAL

Describe a moment when you found yourself competing with a peer. How did this experience shape your understanding of teamwork and collaboration? How did you navigate the situation, and how did this shape your future work relationships?

DAY 45: THE DECEIVER

Write about an instance when you felt manipulated or deceived in a professional setting. How did this experience affect your trust and sense of self?

_____

_____

_____

_____

_____

_____

_____

_____

_____

_____

_____

_____

DAY 46: AUTHENTICITY COMPROMISED

Examine a time when you were tempted to compromise your authenticity to survive in a challenging work environment. What parts of yourself did you have to hide or minimize?

_____

_____

_____

_____

_____

_____

_____

_____

_____

_____

_____

_____

DAY 47: POWER WEAPONS

Recall a situation where you witnessed or experienced power being used as a weapon in the workplace. How did this affect your perception of leadership and professional relationships?

DAY 48: COMPASSIONATE PERSPECTIVE

difficult behavior. What insights did this perspective shift reveal about workplace dynamics?

_____

_____

_____

_____

_____

_____

_____

_____

_____

_____

DAY 49: EXCLUSION EXPERIENCE

Consider a time when you felt like an outsider or were excluded from professional opportunities. How did this experience shape your understanding of workplace power structures and belonging?

EXERCISE: WORKING WITH DIFFICULT PERSONALITIES

When navigating challenging workplace personalities, understanding their motivations can help you respond effectively rather than reactively.

UNDERSTANDING WORKPLACE PERSONALITIES

THE TYRANT

- Often operates from fear and insecurity
- Uses control to mask vulnerability
- May create in-groups/out-groups to maintain power

THE RIVAL

- Deeply competitive, often due to imposter syndrome
- Views success as a zero-sum game
- Struggles with scarcity mindset

THE DECEIVER

- Manipulates situations to maintain control
- Creates cognitive dissonance through gaslighting
- Denies problems or retaliates when confronted

PRACTICAL STRATEGIES

APPROACH WITH COMPASSION

- Remember that difficult behavior typically stems from others' wounds.
- Ask yourself, "What might be driving this behavior?"
- View the person's actions as separate from your worth.

MAINTAIN YOUR CENTER

- Before difficult interactions, ground yourself through breath.
- Respond rather than react by pausing before speaking.
- Mentally prepare with statements such as "This is about them, not me."

SET CLEAR BOUNDARIES

- Determine what behavior you will and won't accept.
- Communicate boundaries calmly and directly.
- Be prepared to walk away from situations that violate your boundaries.

REFLECTION QUESTIONS

1. Which difficult personality affects you most strongly?
2. What trigger patterns do you notice in yourself when dealing with this type?

3. How might compassion change your approach to this person?
4. What specific boundary could you establish in your next interaction?

FEEL FREE TO USE THE FOLLOWING PAGES FOR ANSWERING AND REFLECTING ON THE EXERCISE QUESTIONS

CHAPTER 7

THE GIFT OF MISPERCEPTION
Assessing and Addressing the Ways You're Perceived (Days 50–56)

"Don't think about making women fit the world—
think about making the world fit women."

–Gloria Steinem

DAY 50: BIAS DYNAMICS

Dig deep into a professional moment when unconscious bias shaped how others saw you. What hidden dynamics were at play? How did this experience reshape your understanding of workplace perceptions?

_____

_____

_____

_____

_____

_____

DAY 51: THE PROFESSIONAL MASK

When have you felt like you were wearing a mask at work, hiding your true self to meet others' expectations? Explore the emotional toll of this performance and the parts of yourself you were forced to conceal.

DAY 52: FEEDBACK MIRROR

Imagine you're holding a mirror to a challenging piece of feedback you've received. What initially made you want to turn away? What wisdom might be hiding in the reflection?

DAY 53: MISLABELED SELF

Unpack a professional label that felt like a mismatch for your identity. How did this mischaracterization reveal more about the person labeling you than about yourself?

_____

_____

_____

_____

_____

_____

_____

_____

_____

_____

_____

_____

_____

_____

DAY 54: INVISIBLE BARRIERS

At a moment when you were the outsider in a professional space, what invisible barriers did you encounter? How did these barriers shape your behavior and self-perception?

DAY 55: NARRATIVE ORIGINS

Trace the journey of an internalized narrative about yourself. Where did this story originate? What cultural or personal conditioning breathed life into these perceptions?

_____

_____

_____

_____

_____

_____

_____

_____

_____

_____

_____

DAY 56: CHALLENGING MISPERCEPTIONS

Think of a time you found the courage to challenge a misperception. What inner strength did you draw upon? What did confronting this misunderstanding teach you about your own power and authenticity?

_____

_____

_____

_____

_____

_____

_____

_____

_____

_____

_____

_____

_____

EXERCISE: HANDLING OTHERS' PERCEPTIONS

How others perceive you can be based on bias, partial truth, or valuable feedback. Learning to distinguish between these and respond appropriately is a powerful skill.

THREE TYPES OF PERCEPTIONS

BASED IN BIAS

- Rooted in stereotypes, not your behavior
- Often applied to entire groups (e.g., gender, race)
- Reveals more about perceiver than perceived

CONTAINS KERNELS OF TRUTH

- Has some accuracy but misses context
- May exaggerate a real trait or behavior
- Can provide insight for growth if separated from bias

TRUE AND HARD TO HEAR

- Accurate feedback about blind spots
- Reflects patterns you may not recognize
- Valuable for growth when accepted with grace

PRACTICAL RESPONSE FRAMEWORK

FOR BIAS-BASED PERCEPTIONS:

- Remind yourself: "This is their limitation, not mine."
- Consider whether to address it directly or strategically ignore it.
- Build allies who see beyond stereotypes.

FOR PARTIAL TRUTHS:

- Extract the valuable feedback.
- Identify the contextual factors being missed.
- Address the legitimate concern while clarifying misconceptions.

FOR ACCURATE FEEDBACK:

- Thank the person for their honesty.
- Ask clarifying questions to understand fully.
- Create an action plan for growth.

Reflection Exercise: Think of a recent situation where someone's perception of you felt off. Analyze whether it was based in bias, contained kernels of truth, or was accurate but difficult to hear. Write down the following:

1. The specific perception
2. Which category it falls into and why
3. What response would be most effective
4. What you can learn from this situation

FEEL FREE TO USE THE FOLLOWING PAGES FOR ANSWERING AND REFLECTING ON THE EXERCISE QUESTIONS

CHAPTER 8

WHEN YOU KNOW, YOU KNOW
Finding an Environment Where You Can Thrive (Days 57–63)

> "When you get to a place where you understand that love and belonging, your worthiness, is a birthright and not something you have to earn, anything is possible."
>
> –*Dr. Brené Brown*

DAY 57: IDEAL CULTURE

Envision your ideal workplace culture. What core values would define this environment? How does this vision differ from your current professional reality?

_____

_____

_____

DAY 58: BELONGING MOMENTS

Describe a moment when you felt truly supported and valued at work. What specific elements created that sense of belonging and empowerment?

_____

_____

_____

_____

_____

_____

_____

_____

_____

_____

_____

_____

DAY 59: ENVIRONMENT SIGNALS

Reflect on a time when you recognized that a work environment was no longer serving your growth. What internal and external signals told you it was time to make a change?

_____

_____

_____

_____

_____

_____

_____

_____

_____

_____

_____

DAY 60: UNSPOKEN RULES

Examine the unspoken rules and expectations in your current workplace. How do these implicit norms align or conflict with your personal values and professional aspirations?

DAY 61: INCLUSIVE SPACES

Recall an experience where you witnessed or created a truly inclusive and supportive work environment. What made this space feel different from typical workplace dynamics?

DAY 62: AUTHENTIC COMPROMISES

Consider the compromises you've made to fit into professional spaces. What parts of yourself have you had to minimize or silence? What would it look like to bring your full, authentic self to work?

DAY 63: CAREER CROSSROADS

Write about a professional crossroads where you had to choose between staying in a familiar but limiting environment and stepping into the unknown. What internal dialogue accompanied this decision?

_____

_____

_____

_____

_____

_____

_____

_____

_____

_____

_____

_____

EXERCISE: ENVIRONMENT ASSESSMENT TOOL

Use this tool to evaluate your current work environment and determine if it aligns with your values and needs.

RED FLAGS

- You regularly feel dread before work.
- Your ideas are consistently dismissed or appropriated.
- You've observed patterns of discrimination or microaggressions.
- You find yourself hiding significant parts of your authentic self.
- Physical symptoms (e.g., insomnia, anxiety) related to work appear.
- Promised opportunities repeatedly fail to materialize.

GREEN FLAGS

- You're energized by your work more often than drained.
- Diverse perspectives are actively sought and valued.
- Mistakes are treated as learning opportunities.
- Your contributions are recognized appropriately.
- You can name multiple people who champion your growth.
- The organization's values align with your personal values.

Assessing Alignment: Rate your current environment on these key dimensions (on a scale of 1–10):

- Psychological safety (ability to take risks without fear)
- Value alignment (between personal and organizational values)
- Growth potential (opportunities for advancement and development)
- Authenticity (freedom to be your true self)
- Relationship quality (supportive connections with colleagues)

DECISION FRAMEWORK

- Scores of 8–10: This dimension is thriving.
- Scores of 5–7: This dimension needs attention but may be improvable.
- Scores below 5: Significant misalignment exists in this dimension.

ACTION PLANNING: BASED ON YOUR ASSESSMENT

- Which areas could be improved through conversation and boundary setting?
- Which aspects are nonnegotiable for your well-being?
- What specific changes would make this environment work for you?
- If those changes seem unlikely, what would your exit timeline look like?
- Environments matter. You deserve to be somewhere that recognizes your worth and supports your growth.

FEEL FREE TO USE THE FOLLOWING PAGES FOR ANSWERING AND REFLECTING ON THE EXERCISE QUESTIONS

CHAPTER 9

SURROUND YOURSELF WITH MIRRORS

Building Your Personal Board of Directors (Days 64–70)

> "I feel really grateful to the people who encouraged me and helped me develop. Nobody can succeed on their own."
>
> –Sheryl Sandberg

DAY 64: NETWORK EVOLUTION

Trace the evolution of your professional support network. Who has been a true mirror, reflecting your potential when you couldn't see it yourself?

_____

_____

_____

_____

DAY 65: MENTOR IMPACT

Explore the mentors and sponsors who have shaped your career journey. In what specific ways have these relationships transformed your professional self-understanding?

DAY 66: AUTHENTIC CONNECTIONS

Reflect on a moment when networking felt genuinely empowering rather than transactional. What made that connection feel authentic and meaningful?

DAY 67: SUPPORT GAPS

Describe the gaps in your current professional support system. What types of relationships or perspectives are you missing?

DAY 68: CONNECTION BARRIERS

Examine a time when you hesitated to reach out and ask for professional support. What internal barriers prevented you from building your network?

_____

_____

_____

_____

_____

_____

_____

_____

_____

_____

_____

DAY 69: UNEXPECTED ALLIANCES

Write about a professional relationship that surprised you—someone who became an unexpected ally or supporter.

DAY 70: LIFTING OTHERS

Consider the reciprocity in your professional relationships. How do you lift others up as you climb?

_____

_____

_____

_____

_____

_____

_____

_____

_____

_____

_____

_____

EXERCISE: BUILD YOUR PERSONAL BOARD

A strong personal board of directors provides essential support for your professional journey. Use this exercise to intentionally build yours.

First, here's a recap of the five essential board roles:

LOYAL SUPPORTERS

- Your cheerleaders who believe in you unconditionally
- Safe space for vulnerability and authentic expression
- Remind you of your worth during challenging times

SPONSORS

- Advocate for you in rooms you can't access
- Connect you with opportunities
- Lend their credibility to your advancement

MENTORS

- Provide wisdom from experience
- Offer honest feedback for growth
- Help you navigate professional challenges

ROLE MODELS

- Demonstrate paths you might follow
- Can be people you don't know personally
- Inspire your vision of what's possible

SUBJECT-MATTER EXPERTS

- Provide specialized knowledge
- Offer technical guidance and resources
- Help solve specific challenges

BOARD-BUILDING ACTION STEPS

AUDIT YOUR CURRENT NETWORK

- List who currently serves in each role.
- Identify gaps in representation.
- Note which roles need strengthening.

TARGET NEW CONNECTIONS

- For each gap, identify three potential board members.
- Research their background and areas of expertise.
- Determine mutual connections or entry points.

PLAN YOUR APPROACH

- Craft a specific, authentic reason for connecting.
- Prepare thoughtful questions that show you value their perspective.
- Consider what value you might offer them.

SCHEDULE CONNECTION POINTS

- Set a goal to reach out to one potential board member weekly.
- Create calendar reminders to maintain regular contact.
- Plan for meaningful follow-up after initial meetings.

REFLECTION QUESTIONS

1. Which board role would most affect your current goals if strengthened?
2. What makes you hesitate to reach out to potential board members?
3. How can you be more intentional about nurturing these relationships?

FEEL FREE TO USE THE FOLLOWING PAGES FOR ANSWERING AND REFLECTING ON THE EXERCISE QUESTIONS

_____

_____

_____

_____

_____

CHAPTER 10

MASTER NEGOTIATIONS
Getting What You Want Without Compromising Yourself (Days 71–77)

"Power's not given to you. You have to take it."

–Beyoncé Knowles

DAY 71: ADVOCACY VICTORY

Recall a negotiation where you felt you truly advocated for your worth. What internal resources did you draw upon?

_____

_____

_____

_____

_____

DAY 72: SETTLEMENT PATTERNS

Explore a moment when you settled for less than you deserved in a professional setting. What fears or conditioning drove that compromise?

DAY 73: NEGOTIATION BARRIERS

Describe the invisible barriers that have made negotiating challenging for you. How have gender, race, or cultural expectations shaped your approach?

DAY 74: AUTHENTIC NEGOTIATION

Reflect on a negotiation that felt authentically "you"—where you maintained your integrity while achieving your goals.

DAY 75: VALUE NARRATIVES

Examine the stories you tell yourself about your professional value. How do these internal narratives influence your ability to negotiate?

DAY 76: WALKING AWAY

Write about a time when you walked away from an opportunity that didn't align with your values. What did that decision reveal about your sense of self-worth?

DAY 77: PRINCIPLED FLEXIBILITY

Consider the difference between compromise and capitulation. How do you discern between necessary flexibility and betraying your core principles?

EXERCISE: NEGOTIATION PREP

Successful negotiations require thorough preparation. Use this template before your next important negotiation.

PRENEGOTIATION CHECKLIST

1. DEFINE YOUR DESIRED OUTCOME

- Best-case scenario: _____
- Acceptable outcome: _____
  Walk-away point: _____

2. UNDERSTAND THEIR PERSPECTIVE

- What do they want? _____
- What constraints might they have? _____
- What would make this a win for them? _____

3. IDENTIFY VALUE-ADDING ELEMENTS

- What can you offer that costs you little but benefits them greatly? _____
- How can you frame your request as beneficial to their interests? _____

4. ANALYZE KEY PLAYERS

- Decision-maker(s): _____
- Their priorities: _____

- Potential objections: _____
- How to address each objection: _____

5. SELECT STRATEGY

- Will you start high and compromise? _____
- Will you present your best offer first? _____
- Will you use a relational account? _____
- What specific language will you use? _____

6. CREATE POWER-UP PLAN

- Where will you do your power pose? _____
- What centering technique will you use? _____
- What will you wear to feel confident? _____
- What reminder will you give yourself just before entering?
  _____

REMEMBER

- Enter with clarity but flexibility.
- Focus on creating value for both parties.
- Stay authentic to your communication style.
- Maintain relationships for the long term.

After your negotiation, review what worked and what you'll adjust next time.

FEEL FREE TO USE THE FOLLOWING PAGES FOR ANSWERING AND REFLECTING ON THE EXERCISE QUESTIONS

_____
_____
_____
_____
_____
_____
_____
_____
_____
_____
_____
_____
_____
_____
_____
_____
_____

CHAPTER 11
HARNESS YOUR PRESENCE
Managing Your Energy to Level Up (Days 78–84)

> "Take a stand. Be known for your courage and confidence."
>
> *–Indra Nooyi*

DAY 78: PERFECT ALIGNMENT

Describe a moment when you felt truly aligned—when your inner state and outer performance were in complete harmony.

_____

_____

_____

_____

_____

DAY 79: ENERGY EVOLUTION

Explore how your professional energy has transformed over time. What practices have helped you become more centered and intentional?

_____

_____

_____

_____

_____

_____

_____

_____

_____

_____

_____

_____

_____

DAY 80: ENERGY MANAGEMENT

Reflect on an instance when you consciously managed your energy in a challenging professional situation. What internal shifts occurred?

_____

_____

_____

_____

_____

_____

_____

_____

_____

_____

_____

DAY 81: PROFESSIONAL SELF-CARE

Write about the ways you've learned to protect and nurture your professional spirit. What self-care practices support your most authentic leadership?

_____

_____

_____

_____

_____

_____

_____

_____

_____

_____

_____

DAY 82: RECLAIMING CENTER

Examine a time when external pressures threatened to knock you off your center. How did you find your way back to yourself?

_____

_____

_____

_____

_____

_____

_____

_____

_____

_____

_____

_____

DAY 83: INTERNAL LANDSCAPE

Consider the relationship between your inner landscape and your professional performance. How does your internal state manifest in your work?

_____

_____

_____

_____

_____

_____

_____

_____

_____

_____

_____

_____

DAY 84: FLOW STATE

Describe a moment of professional flow—when your actions felt effortless and your impact was profound. What conditions created that experience?

_____

_____

_____

_____

_____

_____

_____

_____

_____

_____

_____

_____

EXERCISE: ENERGY MANAGEMENT TOOL KIT

Your energy dramatically affects your effectiveness and influence. Use these practices to consciously manage your energy in different situations.

ENERGY CALIBRATION PRACTICES

FOR RAISING YOUR ENERGY

- Power Pose: Stand in an expansive position (wide stance, arms raised or on hips) for two minutes.
- Physical Movement: Do a quick set of jumping jacks, a brisk walk, or stretching.
- Visualization: Picture yourself succeeding brilliantly at the task ahead.
- Powerful Memory: Recall a time when you felt completely in your power.

FOR GROUNDING EXCESS ENERGY

- Belly Breathing: Place one hand on your abdomen and take five deep breaths into your belly.
- Body Scan: Mentally move through your body, releasing tension.
- Present-Moment Focus: Name five things you can see, four you can touch, three you can hear, two you can smell, and one you can taste.
- Physical Grounding: Feel your feet firmly connected to the floor.

ROOM READING GUIDE: BEFORE STRATEGIC MEETINGS OR PRESENTATIONS, ASK YOURSELF THE FOLLOWING

1. What energy level is appropriate for this situation?
2. Who are the key people present, and what energy do they respond to?
3. Do I need to project confidence, warmth, authority, or openness?
4. How can I adjust my energy to create the impact I want?

ENERGY ADJUSTMENT CHALLENGE: THIS WEEK PRACTICE CONSCIOUSLY SHIFTING YOUR ENERGY BEFORE THESE SITUATIONS

- Before an important presentation or meeting
- When entering a challenging conversation
- After receiving difficult news or feedback
- When transitioning between work and home

REFLECTION QUESTIONS

1. When do you feel most energetically aligned and powerful?
2. What situations consistently drain your energy?
3. Which energy management technique feels most effective for you?
4. How does your energy affect those around you?

You can intentionally shift your energy state rather than being at the mercy of your environment or others.

FEEL FREE TO USE THE FOLLOWING PAGES FOR ANSWERING AND REFLECTING ON THE EXERCISE QUESTIONS

CONCLUSION
BE BOLD
Realizing Your Dreams (Days 85–90)

> "Living your best life is your most important journey in life."
>
> –*Oprah Winfrey*

DAY 85: INTEGRATION

Looking back at your workbook entries, what themes, patterns, or insights stand out most strongly? How has your understanding of yourself as a professional evolved?

_____

_____

_____

_____

_____

DAY 86: TRANSFORMATION POINTS

Identify the most significant shifts in your thinking over these past weeks. Which realizations have been most liberating or empowering? Which have been most challenging to accept?

DAY 87: YOUR AUTHENTIC LEADERSHIP

Based on everything you've explored, describe your authentic leadership style. How does this style reflect your core values and unique strengths? How might you continue to refine this style?

_____

_____

_____

_____

_____

_____

_____

_____

_____

_____

_____

DAY 88: YOUR PERSONAL BOARD

Evaluate your personal board of directors. Who has earned their place? Who might you need to add? How will you nurture these relationships going forward?

___
___
___
___
___
___
___
___
___
___
___
___
___

DAY 89: YOUR BOLD VISION

Articulate your bold vision for your professional future. What feels possible now that didn't before? What specific steps will you take to move toward this vision?

_____

_____

_____

_____

_____

_____

_____

_____

_____

_____

_____

_____

_____

DAY 90: YOUR COMMITMENT

Write a letter to your future self, capturing what you've learned and the commitments you're making. What do you want to remind yourself about your power, worth, and potential? How will you continue to show up as your authentic self even when challenged?

EXERCISE: MANIFEST YOUR VISION

As you complete your ninety-day journey, use this exercise to crystallize your vision and set the foundation for bringing it to life.

PART 1: YOUR AUTHENTIC VISION: TAKE TIME TO ENVISION YOUR IDEAL PROFESSIONAL LIFE WITHOUT LIMITATIONS

- What roles would you hold?
- What impact would you make?
- Who would surround you?
- How would you feel each day?
- What values would be expressed through your work?

Write or draw this vision in vivid detail. Include sensory elements—what would you see, hear, and feel in this reality?

PART 2: FROM VISION TO ACTION: TRANSFORM YOUR VISION INTO CONCRETE STEP.

1. **One-Year Milestones:** List three to five achievements that would indicate progress toward your vision.

    o _____
    o _____
    o _____
    o _____
    o _____

2. **Ninety-Day Focus Areas:** Identify two to three key areas to prioritize in the next quarter.

   - _____
   - _____
   - _____

3. **Weekly Practices:** Determine one to two weekly actions that will build momentum.

   - _____
   - _____

4. **Daily Habits:** Choose one daily practice that reinforces your vision.

   - _____
   - _____

PART 3: COMMITMENT RITUAL: CREATE A PERSONAL RITUAL TO FORMALIZE YOUR COMMITMENT TO THIS VISION

- Find a quiet space where you won't be interrupted.
- Read your vision aloud.
- Acknowledge fears or doubts that arise.
- State your commitment to move forward despite them.
- Select a physical object to symbolize this commitment.

FINAL REFLECTION: AS YOU CLOSE THIS WORKBOOK JOURNEY, CONSIDER THE FOLLOWING:

1. How has your understanding of your power evolved?
2. What limited beliefs have you released?
3. What support will you need to maintain momentum?
4. How will you celebrate progress along the way?

You are powerful beyond measure. The journey ahead may not be linear, but with each step forward, you are actively creating the life and career you deserve.

FEEL FREE TO USE THE FOLLOWING PAGES FOR ANSWERING AND REFLECTING ON THE EXERCISE QUESTIONS

_____

_____

_____

_____

_____

_____

FINAL REFLECTIONS

Dear Reader,

As you complete the final reflection in this workbook, I want to acknowledge the significant journey you've undertaken. Over these past ninety days (or however long it's taken you), you've committed to the challenging work of self-discovery, environmental awareness, and personal empowerment. You've examined your triggers, confronted limiting beliefs, recognized patterns, and envisioned new possibilities. This is no small feat—it requires courage, honesty, and persistence.

The insights you've gained through this process belong uniquely to you. They are hard-won treasures that can guide you as you navigate future challenges and opportunities. You now possess a deeper understanding of your authentic self, your true value, and the environments in which you can thrive. Most importantly, you've strengthened your inner compass—the ability to recognize what feels aligned with your values and what doesn't.

Remember that transformation is not a destination but a continuous unfolding. The work you've done here doesn't end with the last exercise. Rather, it has equipped you with tools and perspectives that will continue to serve you throughout your professional and personal life. There will be days when you feel fully in your power and days when you struggle to maintain that connection. This is part of being human.

On the more challenging days, I encourage you to return to this workbook and the accompanying book. Revisit the exercises that resonated most deeply with you. Remind yourself of the insights that felt most liberating or empowering. These pages will remain a resource for you—a place to recalibrate when you feel disconnected from your power or uncertain about your path.

You are now part of a community of individuals who have committed to breaking through their inner glass ceilings and claiming their rightful place at any table they choose. As you move forward, I hope you'll not only continue to advocate for yourself but also to be a mirror, helping to create spaces where others can show up authentically and be valued for their unique contributions.

My deepest wish is that you now recognize, without a doubt, that you are powerful beyond measure. You always have been. May this awareness illuminate your path forward and inspire you to realize your boldest dreams.

Keep Shining,

Sheila

ABOUT THE AUTHOR

Sheila Gujrathi, MD, is a biotech entrepreneur, executive, and champion for women and other underrepresented groups in leadership. Over the past 25 years, she's had the privilege of developing life-changing medicines for patients with serious diseases while building and running multiple biotech companies—including some pretty exciting exits along the way. She currently serves as a chairwoman, board director, strategic advisor, and consultant to many start-up companies and investment funds.

She has taken three biotech companies public and realized multi-billion-dollar acquisitions. Dr. Gujrathi was the co-founder and former CEO of Gossamer Bio and the former Chief Medical Officer of Receptos and has served on multiple company boards as either a Chairwoman or Director. She is currently back to founding and building several biotech companies where she focuses on developing meaningful therapies for patients with high unmet medical needs.

Her journey started at Northwestern University, where she earned both her M.D. and biomedical engineering degree in the accelerated honors program in medical education, and later took her from the academic halls of Harvard Medical School, UCSF, and Stanford to the corporate rooms of world-class companies like McKinsey & Company, Genentech, and Bristol Myers Squibb.

Dr. Gujrathi has earned multiple leadership awards, including AIMBE Fellow, BLOC100 Luminary, Corporate Directors Forum Director of the Year, Healthcare Technology Report Top 25 Women Leaders in Biotechnology, Athena Pinnacle Award, and Endpoints 20 Biopharm R&D and was named among the Fiercest Women in Life Sciences. But what really lights her up? Creating the kind of supportive, inclusive environments she wished she'd had throughout her career. That's why she co-founded the Biotech CEO Sisterhood, a group of transformative trailblazing female CEOs, and the South Asian Biopharma Alliance—because she believes we're all better when we lift each other up.

When she's not working to bring new therapies to patients or mentoring the next generation of leaders, you'll find her at home with her family, trying to keep up with her teenagers' latest adventures.